Signs in My World

Signs on the Road

By Mary Hill

Welcome Books™

Children's Press®
A Division of Scholastic Inc.
New York / Toronto / London / Auckland / Sydney
Mexico City / New Delhi / Hong Kong
Danbury, Connecticut

Photo Credits: Cover and all photos by Maura B. McConnell
Contributing Editor: Jennifer Silate
Book Design: Erica Clendening and Michelle Innes

Library of Congress Cataloging-in-Publication Data

Hill, Mary, 1977—
    Signs on the road / by Mary Hill.
    p. cm. — (Signs in my world)
    Summary: A young boy in a wheelchair and his mother drive to go shopping,
    observing the various road signs on the way including the handicapped parking
    sign, which shows them where to park close to the store.
    ISBN 0-516-24270-9 (lib. bdg.) — ISBN 0-516-24362-4 (pbk.)
    1. Traffic signs and signals—Juvenile literature. [1. Traffic signs
    and signals. 2. People with disabilities.] I. Title. II. Series.

TE228 .H54 2003
625.79'4—dc21
                            2002007209

Contents

1 Driving to the Store   4

2 Stop Sign   6

3 One Way Sign   10

4 New Words   22

5 To Find Out More   23

6 Index   24

7 About the Author   24

My name is Ethan.

Mom is going to **drive** us to
the store.

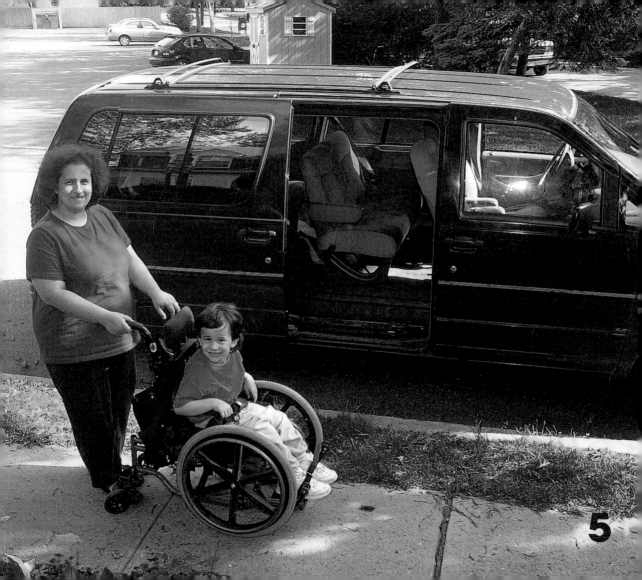
5

There are many **signs** on the road.

The first sign we see is a Stop sign.

The Stop sign tells **drivers** to stop their cars.

Mom stops our car at the Stop sign.

Look, there is another sign.

It says, "One Way."

The One Way sign tells drivers which **direction** to go.

The cars must only go in the direction shown on the sign.

ONE WAY

13

This yellow sign has a picture of a person on it.

15

The yellow sign tells drivers that people may want to **cross** the street.

Mom stops the car so people can cross.

17

This sign has a picture of a
person in a **wheelchair**.

It tells us that only
people with a **handicap**
can **park** there.

Mom parks our car by
the sign.

We are parked close to the store.

Parking close to the store makes it easier for me to get there.

It is time to go **shopping**.

New Words

cross (**krawss**) to go from one side to the other

direction (duh-**rek**-shuhn) the way that someone or something is moving

drive (**drive**) to control a vehicle

drivers (**drive**-urz) people who control vehicles

handicap (**han**-dee-kap) an illness or injury that makes it difficult to do certain things, such as walking

park (**park**) to leave a car in a space

shopping (**shop**-ing) going to stores to buy goods

signs (**sinez**) public notices that give information

wheelchair (**weel**-chair) a chair with wheels for people who cannot walk

To Find Out More

Books
Red, Yellow, Green: What Do Signs Mean?
by Joan Holub
Cartwheel Books

Road Signs: A Harey Race with a Tortoise
by Margery Cuyler
Winslow Press

Web Site
Tex and Dot's Kid's Page
http://www.dot.state.tx.us/kidsonly/texanddotpg/kidspage.html
Learn about road signs and much more on this informative Web site.

Index

cross, 16

drive, 4
drivers, 8, 12, 16

handicap, 18

park, 18, 20

shopping, 20
Stop sign, 6, 8

wheelchair, 18

About the Author
Mary Hill writes and edits children's books.

Reading Consultants
Kris Flynn, Coordinator, Small School District Literacy, The San Diego County Office of Education

Shelly Forys, Certified Reading Recovery Specialist, W.J. Zahnow Elementary School, Waterloo, IL

Sue McAdams, Former President of the North Texas Reading Council of the IRA, and Early Literacy Consultant, Dallas, TX